T0193611

UNDERSTANDING NARRATIVE INQUIRY THROUGH PERSONAL EXPERIENCE.

Administration & Teaching in Nunavut, Canada

Kurt C. Donald (M. Ed.)

Balboa Press books may be ordered through booksellers or by contacting:

Balboa Press
A Division of Hay House
1663 Liberty Drive
Bloomington, IN 47403
www.balboapress.com
844-682-1282

ISBN: 979-8-7652-2686-5 (sc)
ISBN: 979-8-7652-2687-2 (e)

Print information available on the last page.

Balboa Press rev. date: 04/06/2022

TABLE OF CONTENTS

DEDICATION

This book is dedicated to my late father who passed away suddenly on November 17th, 2019, at the Saint John Regional Hospital in Saint John, NB. My father was the most kind-hearted, giving, and loving father any son could ask for. When I think of my dad, I am often reminded of the song by Zac Brown Band called My Old Man. That song resonates with me and is everything that I ever saw in my father.

I also would like to dedicate this book to my mother who has been through a lot of traumas since the passing of her husband. She loved her husband with all her heart and being. They were each other's first loves and were married for over 60 years. There is not a day goes by that she does not think of him.

ACKNOWLEDGEMENTS

I would like to dedicate this book to my current supervisor, Mr. Chris Snow who is the principal of the school that I currently work at in Baker Lake, Nunavut. Without him hiring me for this position I would not have had the experiences that I have had working with the amazing Inuit and non-Innuit staff at the school, not to mention learning the Inuit culture from the students that I teach. Mr. Snow's guidance and leadership has helped me develop and hone my skills to become the educator that I am today and for that I could not be more grateful. His nickname from me is "Dawg" and I give him that name as a sign of complete and total respect of the highest level.

INTRODUCTION

These four narrative stories are from my personal and professional experience (utilizing the narrative genre of autobiography) that have happened during my career as an educator in Nunavut. Narrative is a form of research (Wilson, 2008) and as Kim (2016) posits, "Telling stories is the primary way we express what we know and who we are" (p. 9). I share these stories as a way of further understanding self as well as how to show empathy and understanding from a personal and professional perspective. Clandinin & Connelly (1994) explain:

> Methods for the study of personal experience are simultaneously focused in four directions: inward and outward, backward, and forward. By inward we mean the internal conditions of feelings, hopes, aesthetic reactions, moral dispositions and so on. By outward, we mean existential conditions, that is, the environment…By backward and forward we are referring to temporality, past, present, and future. To experience an experience is to experience that simultaneously in these four ways and to ask questions pointing each way. (p. 417)

My positionality when authoring these stories come from who and what I am as a person and researcher; this identity includes respect, trust, kindness, love, and integrity. Contributions to these stories include a strong sense of open-mindedness, willingness to learn from these events as they transform and inform my life, as well as a yearning to share these personal stories and knowledge with others. I am a qualitative researcher, a 51-year-old, heterosexual, agnostic, white Canadian male, coming from a middle-class background. I was born and raised in Sackville, NB, a small university/retirement town on the East Coast of New Brunswick (Sackville, NB). I am currently a PhD student at Cambridge University in Boston, Mass. USA; I work as a middle school math and health teacher that works in a small fly-in isolated community in the territory of Nunavut, in the Hamlet of Baker Lake.

Losing My Dad During My PhD Journey While Teaching in Nunavut

It was cold and dark even at this time of the morning, November 17th, 2019. It was 10:25 am when I was suddenly awakened by the ringing of my mobile phone by my bedside. Startled and groggy, I turned over to my right, grabbed the phone, and answered it. Strangely it was my mom on the other end which was out of sorts for her as she never usually calls in the morning hours unless it is urgent. I said hello and she said in a shaky, feeble voice, "I have some unwelcome news. He is gone." I immediately bolted up on the side of the bed and said, "What do you mean he is gone? Who is he?" She replied, "Dad, he is gone. He is dead." Shocked, dismayed and in total disbelief I said, What? What do you mean he is dead? What happened?" She went on to explain that his heart stopped. Doctors managed to restart his heart once and it stopped again, they revived him, and second time and it stopped again. The third time was not successful and he flatlined and was pronounced dead.

Luckily when my mom called me, she had family with her and at least that part was comforting to me. Her sister Nancy took the phone from Mom and all I heard Mom say to the others with her in the room was, "The doctors said he is coming home tomorrow." I then knew she was in shock and denial. My aunt (Nancy) told me that I needed to come home right away and so I began making flight arrangements to come back to New Brunswick from Nunavut.

When I finally hung up the phone I sat on my bedside in total shock and disbelief that this had happened. My Dad was always in perfect health and at 84 years of age, had never been admitted to hospital once in his life. Knowing this and thinking about what I had just found out make me stop and think about just how precious and unpredictable life can be and you never know when the gift of life and living can be taken away from you at moment's notice. I sat on my bedside and began to cry uncontrollably. My life had suddenly come to a screeching halt and everything the way I had known nit just 24-hours prior to this even had now and forever would be changed forever.

Once the flight arrangements had been made (I had to wait two days before I could get out of the fly-in community where I live) I began my journey home. The time that it took me to get home seemed like forever. A neighbour of ours picked me up from the airport. They greeted me with open arms and plenty of tears were shed. The drive from the airport home, although it seemed like forever, was less than 30 minutes.

When the car finally pulled up to my mom's apartment, I noticed that inside was full of family. I sat in the car for the longest time not wanting to face my new reality. When I tried to move my legs to get out of the car, I could not move at all. It was as if my legs had been frozen stiff; they felt like two pieces of hard cement. I began to cry profusely. Finally, I was able to move and slowly went to the apartment door. When I opened it, my mom got up out of her chair and came over to me. We hugged, cried, and cried together for the longest time while other in the room sat silently with tears streaming down their faces. That night was long, dark and the pain was felt to my inner core.

The following days were almost surreal. I simply could not imagine that this had happened and yet it did. I was informed that my dad was going to be cremated and that I should go to the funeral home and pay my respects and to say my final goodbye to him.

It was a cold, damp, dark morning in November in Sackville, NB. The air was dense and filled with extreme sadness all around me. Upon entering the funeral home, I was told that my dad was behind the set of doors and the back and once I opened them, he would be there. The walk to the back of the room where he lay took forever to get there. My legs were shaking. I was clammy with perspiration and my legs felt that they were once again like cement pillars as before. I barely had enough strength to open the door as my hands were like two pieces of ice. Upon opening the door, I was shocked at what I saw. My dad was lying there, lifeless, arms folded over, hand over hand. I remember seeing his hands rough-like and cracked as my dad had a hard life growing up. When I looked at his face, apart from him not wearing his glasses, he looked exactly like he always did. Hair cut short and combed over and always neat and professional looking. He had a very peaceful aura about him. He was at peace. I cried and cried and cried. We had a conversation for about five minutes or so where I told him he was the best father ever I thanked him for all he had given me in my life and that I loved him with all my heart. I also made the promise to him that I would look after mom just like they had done for all the years of my life. I turned, said one final I love you and shut the door behind me. He was later cremated that same day.

This experience has taught me the value of life and to never take it for granted. It has also taught me to always be thankful every single day of your life for what you have as you never know when any or all of it can be taken away from you at a moment's notice or with no notice at all. As I write this, I am remined of a saying that I read as a tattoo on an individual's arms that read, "Life is a journey, not a destination." And along each of our journeys we never know what may happen unexpectedly. Life is not predictable; it is the complete opposite. To add to this Kim (2016) posits that, "Because we understand our own lives in terms of the narratives that we live out and share, narrative is appropriate for understanding the actions of others" (p. 8). It is my hope that when others read this story about the death of my father that they too can relate and feel the same shock and pain that I did and to know that they are not alone; that all of us as humans experience painful and traumatic events in our lives as this is part of life.

This experience has changed my personal life as I take the time to now stop and "smell the roses;" I do not ignore them or take for granted that these beautiful flowers will always be where they are at any given moment in time. In other words, I appreciate my life more now than I ever have before and I am cherishing the time now that I have left with my mom as she is elderly (87 years old). I value time and the importance of it in relation to my life and the lives of others around me. And Kim (2016), further explains that "By way of storytelling, we allow stories to travel from person to person, letting the meaning of story become larger than an individual experience and an individual life" (p. 9). This is exactly what I am hoping for in the telling of this personal story about the unexpected death of my father; that this tragic event, others can relate to and share their experiences with others they know and know that they are not alone. Also, Kim (2016) further posits that "Telling stories is the primary way we express what we know and who we are" (p. 9). Further to this, the telling of my story proves that we are all connected to one another through life and death situations and that tragedies such as this are not only part of my lived experience, but the lived experience of others too.

This specific time of my dad's passing is significant as I believe now, after reflecting and trying to heal through this tragedy, that it may have just been his time to 'go;' that his "work" on Earth was complete and it was time for him to move onward to his next journey. The reason I say this is that my mom told me that at church, "he was getting closer to his time and his peace and learnings from God." I believe these observations to be true. Even so, I still wish that he were here physically with my mom and me. However, I do know that he is still here with us in spirit.

The aftermath of the death of my father and life goes on – Concluding Thoughts

My father passed away November 17th, 2019. After arriving home two days later (as I could not get a flight out of Baker Lake until then), the apartment where my mom and dad had been living for the past 10 years suddenly felt cold and dark, with a sense of emptiness within its four walls. The remainder of the evening after arrival was spent with family and close friends as they dropped by the apartment to express their sadness and deepest condolences for our loss. Later that same night something very strange happened to me as I made my way to bed for the night.

When I finally climbed into bed and shut the lights out, I lay there with tears streaming down my cheeks. I was still in denial that this had just happened and could not understand why it happened and why we deserved to be put through this agony, pain, and misery we were experiencing. Laying still, I tried to close my eyes and go to sleep as I was physically and mentally exhausted from flying home and having to endure the pain that followed once I crossed the threshold into my parent's apartment door. As I lay there my mind kept wondering why this had happened and so quickly too. My dad had never been in a hospital a single day in his life, and he was 84 years of age. He was healthy or so we all had thought anyway. I could not sleep as my eyes simply would not shut and my brain would not shut off from this traumatic event that had just transpired. As I was trying to get comfortable and relax, for some reason I looked up toward the upper right portion of the ceiling in my bedroom (as if I were drawn or made to look there for a reason I did not know at that moment). It was as if I was tapped on the shoulder and asked to do so. As I began to look upward, to my surprise I saw a miniature version of my dad hanging steadily in mid-air. I blinked again as I thought my mind was playing tricks on me due to exhaustion, but as I did the picture of him remained there. I began to cry uncontrollably. My dad then said to me, "Kurt, I need you to stop crying and do not worry. I am in a better place now. What I need you to do for me is two things. First and most importantly, please look after your mother and take care of her for me. Second, please take care of yourself and do not give up on your studies. Keep going! As I have taught you all along, never give up on

7

something you started. See it through until completion. Make your mom and I even more proud of you than we already are." With that said, I replied, "Ok. Consider it done. I will not let you down dad. I love you always." After I spoke those final four words to him the image disappeared, and the room went into total darkness once more. After this I was then able to settle, relax and finally drift off to sleep.

The next few days, weeks, and months were very uneasy and difficult for me to deal with. I was worried about my mom as she was not herself and her behaviours were completely out of character for her. She would get up several times in the middle of the night and sit in the living room in total darkness for hours on end. She would often say things that made little sense or were very hurtful towards me, and even though I knew deep down that she did not mean them, they were still difficult to hear. I stayed at home with my mom until after the Christmas break when I had to go back to work.

The months that followed until summer break I stayed in contact with mom on a regular basis, about once or twice every couple of weeks just to see how she was coping. With the help of family and friends visiting her, she endured and coped as best as possible despite the circumstances. When it was time to come home for the summer again, I could not wait to get home and to be with her again. That summer I helped her as much as I could both mentally by being home so that she was not alone, and financially with her rent and nurses helped her. Everything was going as well as could be expected until two days before I had to leave for back to work at the end of the summer.

Mom had decided that one morning she was going to go strawberry picking with friends of hers for the morning. I thought it was a great idea for her to get out and to socialize with her friends and to get some summer fresh air too. While she was away, I was busy with my online year 1 PhD course until another tragedy struck last minute.

As I was online, the friend that she went strawberry picking with came to my bedroom door and knocked. I got up and opened the door only to be told that while picking strawberries my mom had fallen and broke her leg or so she thought. I cannot even begin to explain what was going through my head at that moment. I thought, how could this happen? What did my mom or I do to deserve all this pain and anguish? Why was there such an intense 'black cloud' above our heads for this to happen? Was the death of my dad not enough pain for us to endure? Her friend proceeded to tell me that they were taking her to outpatients for x-rays and would let me know what was going on once they found out.

Hours and hours went by before I finally got the telephone call and the news that I knew was not going to be good. Her friend told me that her leg was broken quite badly and that she would need to go to the city hospital and have it operated on as quickly as possible. I was in shock and complete denial and disbelief once more. As if the death of my father was not bad enough. And now this! Not to mention that this happened two days before I was to leave for back to Nunavut. Mom told me that I had to go and not to worry that she would get the care and help she required. Taking her advice, I left for Nunavut two days later with such a heavy heart and guilty conscience feeling as though I was leaving and deserting her when she was injured.

These experiences have taught me that life cannot be predetermined or predicted, and that life as I know it at the time, can change at a moments' notice without any warning. And as Polkinghorne (1988), cited in Kim (2016), with regards to research into meaning it is "the most basic of all inquiry" (p. 190). Further to this, Polkinghorne (1988) explains that narrative meaning:

1. Functions to give form to the understanding of a purpose to life and to join everyday actions and events into episodic units; (2) provides a framework for understanding the past events of one's life and for planning future actions; and is the primary scheme by means of which human existence is rendered meaningful. (p. 191)

It is my intention that when others read this story about the death of my father and the aftermath of such an experience as well as dealing with the injury of a frail mother with the breaking of her leg, that readers can relate to my experience and have similar feelings that I did when dealing with such unexpected and live altering moments and that these are all part of what is called life.

This experience has changed my personal life as I do not take anything in life for granted and take the time to spend with my mom and let nothing get in the way of that. Nussbaum (1998), cited in Kim (2016), explains that "The ability to think what it might be like to be in the shoes of a person different from oneself, to be an intelligent reader of that person's story, and to understand the emotions and wishes and desires that someone so placed might have" (p. 228). This is what I am hoping in the telling of my personal stories about the death of my father and the unexpected fall of my mother; those other readers can relate to and reflect on their experience(s) too when dealing with elderly parents. The telling of my story illustrates that life is precious and we never know what is going to happen from one day to the next or one minute to the next for that matter. I also hope that my experience will show that when tragedy occurs, we must deal with it as best as we can as life does not stop, that life continues whether our loved ones are with us at the time or not.

This specific time of these difficulties in my life, is relevant to where I am now in my own life. At mid age (51 years old) I now realize what is most important in life. It is not what you have, what you own, or what you can buy, instead it is all about living and living life to the fullest possible and not taking anything that life has provided me for granted, especially when it comes to my family.

The Suicide That Changed My Life Forever

It was October 2006, 2:05 am. The phone rang unexpectedly, and both my wife and I were startled by ring. My wife heard it first and was closest to the phone on the bedside nightstand. Groggy, she answered the phone. She handed me the receiver and told me that it was my boss from the school. My heart sank to my feet and began to beat like I had just completed a marathon race. I knew it could only be shocking news. My boss proceeded to inform me that a student of mine who I was remarkably close with as we had established a solid rapport since I had her for math in grade 6, 7 and now in grade 8. He went on to tell me that the fire department had not long ago found her hanging from a tree branch behind the hockey arena. I began to sob uncontrollably, so much so that my wife was worried I was going to have a heart attack. He then told me there would be a debriefing at the school in the conference room at the school in the morning. I mumbled with tears in my eyes and heavy breathing that I would be there. For the rest of the early morning hours, I did not go back to sleep. I sat on the bedside for the longest time, emotionless, numb inside and no energy or ability to do anything. It was as if this new had completely paralysed me both mentally and physically. My wife tried to console me, but it was moot in effectiveness. I just wanted to be left alone to try and process what I had just learned. She let me be for the rest of the night.

In the morning, I slowly and unwillingly got ready for work. Every movement of my body and every thought in my mind made me weaker and weaker to the point where I did not think I could go to work, yet I knew I had to as that is what the student would have wanted. And so, I did just that.

Once at the school I sat in my car for the longest time trying to get my mind to focus on what was ahead of me once I entered the school. Getting out of the car, my legs felt like rubber. The air was cold, damp, and gloomy, how fitting. Upon entering the school, I got an immediate chill that ran down my back. No one was in sight at that moment. I shakily and slowly walked down my corridor to my classroom and unlocked the door. The first thing my eyes went to be the seat in the middle of the first row where she always sat. She always wanted to sit up front, closest to the board so that she could learn everything that I was about to teach. Her brain was like a sponge. She absorbed everything I taught her. She was an exemplary student, having won the grade 7 cash award for the highest average in grade 7 math. I walked to my desk and sat down with a sigh of relief that I made it that far. From this moment I began to cry uncontrollably. I was then consoled in my classroom by a few teachers who had dropped by my room when they heard me sobbing. At this point before school started for the day, I general assembly debriefing meeting was called, and all staff were to meet in the conference room.

Once I got to the conference room and stepped through the doorway the air seemed thick and dense with sadness and grief. People were holding hands, hugging each other, and crying uncontrollably. It was a horrific experience to be a part of. At the meeting, details of what we had already known were gone over once more so that everyone knew exactly who it was that had taken their life, what occurred, where it occurred, and how it occurred. The only huge question that remained was why it occurred? That was the million-dollar question that no one had any answer to until later when more details come to the surface and were verified.

Later, in the day we learned the reason(s) as to why this had happened. Her homeroom teacher and I went looking for clues, so we started by looking through her homeroom desk as this was the desk where she sat for ELA (English Language Arts). We did not find any supporting evidence in her desk to sound the alarm as to the reason this had happened. However, after looking and the graffiti and what was written on her desk, we found overwhelming evidence that she was hurting and thought that she had no one to trust and no one could help her with what she was going through. She was experiencing severe trauma at home. This evidence was later confirmed by the RCMP. What we found out was that her mom's boyfriend was physically and sexually abusing her while her mom was at work. This was the reason she always wanted to stay behind after school and did not want to go home even when our day was done, and we were leaving. Initially we thought that she just liked hanging out at the school and being around her teachers. There was no clear, visible evidence that she was being abused and if there was, she hid the evidence well. We also learned that this had been going on for over two years without her mother even knowing, let alone suspecting that this was occurring in the same household where all three of them were living. It was devasting news for all of us to learn and I even blamed myself at one point for not being as aware as I should have been that something was going on with her at home. Yet she always functioned as though her life was going well while at school. She was always full of laughter, always smiling and always ready and willing to learn and to take on any challenge that was set out before her. The saddest part about all of this besides losing a smart, young, and capable Aboriginal student was that even though her mom found out about what her boyfriend had been doing to her daughter while she was away at work, the boyfriend and mother continued to live together after the fact as though nothing had ever happened except that they had lost their daughter to suicide! This event still haunts me to this very day, these many years later.

This experience has taught me that you never know what is going on in the personal lives of my students; those students have a way of "covering up" what goes on at home and can do this well, and without being noticed that they are experiencing trauma. This experience has also taught me that as educators we need to be vigilant when it comes each students' life and to ask questions about their wellbeing where appropriate. We also need to be mindful that it is not just our job to teach, but to also be mentors and show care, empathy, and a willingness to help when needed. Kim (2016) explains that "Narrative Inquiry presumes the importance of the everyday, the ordinary, the quotidian stories that have frequently gone unnoticed" (p. 23). Suicide, especially with Aboriginal youth always seems go unnoticed or the attitude of "it's just another Aboriginal youth" that took their own life; that these tragedies seem to become the norm and often their stories as to why they did what they did become "back page" news stories. Therefore, it is important according to Shields (2005), cited in Kim (2016), that "Sharing stories involves reconstructing stories from the past in the light of present knowledge. It is not enough to tell the same story in the same way across time if that story is to be used to connect with new meaning and inform us in the present" (p. 180). Therefore, these tragedies need to be further analysed using current research to connect the past to the present; that this has been going on for a prolonged period and links need to be made between the past and the present to get to the root cause(s) of why these things happen in the first place. This is also why as narrative researchers; temporality is important when we think and write as we need to link these past tragedies to the present and to project outcomes for the future.

This experience has changed my personal life in that I now value the life that I am living and try to show as much empathy as I can towards those that may be experiencing this type of trauma in their own lives. And as Nussbaum (1998), cited in Kim (2016) posits, "that story about others that we read through literature can help us cultivate narrative imagination that enlarges our empathetic understanding" (p. 112). I see the value in life and the preciousness of it, but this is coming from a non-Aboriginal lens. I need to try more to view these tragedies through an Aboriginal lens to better understand the issues that are facing them on a day-by-day basis.

This experience has changed my professional life as I am now more aware of the struggles of my Indigenous students and need to show understanding, patience, empathy and be willing to take the time to listen more and speak less. Listening is an important theme in Indigenous culture and needs to always be respected.

This specific time was of importance as this student meant the world to me. She was kind, caring, and academically brilliant. Also, following her death, this created a suicide "snowball effect" where we had nine suicides back-to-back in our community. It was a sad, dark, gloomy time in my life as an educator. It was a traumatic, painful time in my life and still affects me today. Even where I am working right now, this past year I experienced five students who took their life, one a potential graduating student for this year.

I have learned that experiencing these tragedies and dealing with the trauma of each, that no matter our race, gender, religious affiliation, sexual orientation, and so forth we are all human beings. We all have feelings, thoughts, opinions, and diverse ways to express ourselves which makes us unique and different from one another. And as the saying goes, "Variety is the spice of life" and I could not agree more.

The aftermath following the suicide of one of my students: How this changed my life both personally and professionally forever

In 2007 while working as a math teacher at a First Nations school I received the horrifying news that one of my best grade 8 math students had committed suicide. This event and the days that followed changed my life both on a personal and a professional level forever.

I received the news of the suicide by phone in the middle of the night by my administrator. That night was filled with tears, sadness, emptiness, and a feeling as though I had let this student down in some way, that I did not see the signs before it was too late.

The next morning while getting ready for work, I was slower than normal, as if I wanted to be purposely late for work or better yet not go at all. But I know that that is not what my student would have wanted. She would want me to go despite what had happened and to keep going.

Once at the school I slowly walked to the entrance and walked in. The air in the school had an eerie, almost haunted, heavy feeling about it, like walking into a morgue. I walked to my classroom door and opened it, turned on the lights only to see empty seats, but one seat caught my eye more than the others. It was the seat that would remain empty from this day forward forever. The seat was in the middle of the first row where she always sat, closest to the chalkboard. She was an excellent math student. I went to my desk, took off my coat and sat down in my chair and sat with complete disbelief that this had just happened. After a few minutes of just sitting there, motion-less, there was a call for a debriefing meeting and all staff were to meet in the conference room.

It was here that I learned why this had happened. She was experiencing severe trauma at home (sexual abuse by her mother's boyfriend). When the debriefing was over, it was time to start the day with the students. They all arrived as they normally did. Some came with appropriate clothing, others did not. Some came with breakfast in their tummies, others did not. The one observation that I did make though is that it was as if this tragedy was not a big deal, that she was just another statistic, another number to add to the growing number of suicides of First Nations peoples. Even the students of her class did not seem to be that upset when they came to my classroom. The tone and atmosphere of the class was sombre and quiet, but that was the only difference this time.

As I was waiting for all the students to arrive and take their seats, I kept my eye on that one almost separate from the others, the one seat that stood out in my eyes from all the others, the seat that would not be filled by the bubbly, funny, smart student that was supposed to occupy it. Finally, the last student arrived and as always was late for class or was the last student to enter before the bell rang. I did not have a positive relationship with this student. I tried to establish rapport with him but just could not. We just did not click on any level. As he walked in slowly, as he always did, instead of going to his regular seat at the back of the classroom, next to my desk, he decided to sit down at the front where 'she' used to sit. When he sat down, I became enraged with anger. I took the loss of one of my students out on him in front of the entire class. Immediately afterwards, I thought, "What did I just do?"

The remainder of the class did not go particularly well as one can imagine. Students were upset with me that I scolded one of their classmates in front of them and who could blame them for that matter. It was not his fault that this happened, and he was not to blame for the events that took place. After this, I went and sat at my desk with utter disgust in myself for what I had just said and done to this student. I had automatically assumed that he sat in her seat to try and get a 'rise' out of me and to disrespect me as he and the rest of the class knew that she was one of my favourite students in the class. I knew that I had to make this right some way, somehow, and before the end of the day.

At the end of the period, students went on their way to the next class. I was still full of shame and guilt as my next class came in. I kept thinking about how I was going to try and repair the damage that I had done with this student as I had used my big mouth to create this issue and I knew that I had thoroughly put my also big foot square in it.

As the end of the day approached, when the final bell rang, I asked if I could speak to the student that I had so rudely spoken to come and speak with me after school in my classroom. When asked to, he was hesitant and I could tell was a bit scared too, but nonetheless he did. I started off the conversation by telling him how incredibly sorry I was for doing what I did and that I should never have said the things I did to him in front of his peers. I went on to explain that my raw emotions got the best of me and instead of stepping back for a moment to analyse the situations it was unfolding, I overreacted and said what I did to him. I told him I said those things not because I meant it for him specifically, but because at that moment he was taking up the space in the chair of the student that meant the world to me. I told him it was as if he were almost sitting on top of her as I still was picturing her sitting there (even though she was not) and would never be again. I humbly and with great humility apologized and told him that I should not have said what I did or acted the way I did and that it was not meant to be directed at him. I told him that I was going through a tremendous amount of pain at that moment, but at the same time my actions and behaviours were uncalled for and were also unprofessional too. I asked him to forgive me for what I said and in doing so the tears came streaming down my cheeks. He also teared up and said that all was ok and to just forget what had happened today and that tomorrow is a new day. We shook hands and he left and went home.

This experience has taught me that each of us have our limits and ways that we deal with things, especially when it comes to the trauma that suicide brings. This suicide was just one of many that have occurred in this community, and even one, is too many. As educators we have the ability and power to cause remarkable things to happen as well as to create trauma in many of these students lives, even more so than what they are dealing with on a regular basis. As an educator I need to be mindful of the words that come out of my mouth and the way that I express myself to students. I need to take the time to step back, reflect, and then speak. Without doing this can create even more trauma for students to endure. Kim (2016) explains that Narrative inquiry can link "readers to a sphere of possible contact with a developing, incomplete and evolving situation, allowing them to re-think and re-evaluate their own views, prejudices, and experiences." (p. 235). This is also why I believe that storytelling as part of narrative is so vital in qualitative research and as Kim (2016) further explains, "Narrative inquiry is a quest for knowledge about one's life through narrative" (p. 236).

Indigenous peoples have developed storytelling traditions over the years that have come to include the various ways that Indigenous storytelling can be viewed as a form of both teaching and learning as well as an expression of Aboriginal culture and identity (Wilson, 2008). Little Bear (2014) explains, "Education and socialization are achieved through praise, reward, recognition, and renewal ceremonies and by example, actual experience, and storytelling" (p. 81). He further posits that, "Storytelling is a very important part of the education process. It is through stories that customs and values are taught and shared" (p. 82).

This experience has changed my professional life in how I deal with students in times of community crisis like suicide. I now realize that I must show as much empathy as I can to all students that are affected by events such as this one. I need to view these tragedies through my Indigenous lens to try and further understand how these issues affect my students. I also realize the importance and value in developing rapport and trust with all my students, and to keep trying if the endeavour fails. I had a supervisor tell me that developing rapport with students starts on the first day of school and stops the last day of school. It took me many years to figure out what he meant by this, but I now know and am mindful of my duties as an educator to not just teach, but to provide empathy, and develop trust, but to also develop positive, long-lasting relationships with all my students. And as Little Bear (2014) explains, "Children are greatly valued and are considered gifts from the Creator." (p. 81). Wilson (2008) states, "If we step outside the community of Indigenous scholars, we can see the importance of relationship building in the everyday lives of most Indigenous people" (p. 84). He further explains that "Shared relationships allow for a strengthening of the new relationship. This allows you to become familiar or comfortable with the person" (p. 84).

15

Looking back on what I said and the way I said it, I still remember this as if it happened yesterday. I still feel shame for doing what I did. However, it was a lesson that I learned the hard way. And as Kim (2016) states, "By deconstructing the way we internalize past events, we sometimes painfully open wounds in an attempt to cleanse and purify so that strength and endurance can emerge" (p. 255). I think that this event, as unprofessional as it was at the time, has made me stronger and better able to cope with tragedies such as this. This I believe is the power of narrative inquiry in research. And according to Pinar, et al. (2008), cited in Kim (2016), the focus of autobiographical narratives is that "they should create a new future through the transformative opening of wounds. The deconstructive process is where we move ourselves inward, outward, forward, backward, diagonally, and circularly to find our being." (p. 255). I have learned that experiencing any kind of trauma influences everyone else too, and that this is part of what is meant by being human.

> It was February 2019. It was a frigid day at -50 Celsius. The students from the middle school wing of the school were invited down to the atrium (cafeteria) to take part in the cultural learning of how to properly skin and prepare a muskox. The teachers, I included, had some trepidation about bringing all the students from two grades 8 and two grade 9 classes together for this event, reason being is that there were a few students in this group that had severe behaviour issues, and could not congregate together without these behaviours becoming an issue. We made it clear however before they went downstairs that we expected good behaviour and those that did not comply would be sent to the principal's office to not ruin the learning event for everyone else that wanted to take part.

Once downstairs and settled, several Elders and a few younger adults began to explain what was going to happen. They explained the significance of why these animals are prepared the way that they are to not waste what Creator has provided for everyone for sustenance purposes. They explained that nothing is wasted and that all parts of the muskox have a purpose. They also explained that if this were to be done out on the land that the legs of the muskox would be placed together and left out on the land as a way of saying thanks for providing this nourishment for everyone.

Much to all our disbelief, we could not believe how well behaved all the students were during this time, which was about two hours in length. Every student was engaged in the cultural learning that was happening; every student had at least one question that they asked the Elders and young adults who were doing the demonstration for us; every student was learning in real time together, with no behaviour issues at all.

When the demonstration was over, and we went back to the classroom we discussed the experience and what they had learned. I was utterly shocked at what they had told me. Many commented on the fact that what they witnessed is part of the Inuit ways of knowing, knowing exactly how to skin and prepare the muskox. Many shared their own experiences being out on the land with their fathers and grandfathers in how they skinned and prepared other animals such as caribou as an example. They also shared how much they enjoyed the learning experience and requested that more of this type of learning should take place at the school. I wrote down their suggestions and gave their feedback to administration to take into consideration for future learning events like this one. It was an afternoon that I would not forget, and neither would my students as they still talk about the skinning of the muskox to this day!

This experience has taught me that when it comes to the culture of Inuit youth, they view these traditional Inuit ways of knowing how to skin and properly prepare a muskox, these students are actively engaged in the learning process and are actively willing to learn when the learning is relatable to them and their culture.

This experience has changed my professional life as I now do not judge students as much as I used to base on their behaviour plans. I once read "that there is no such thing as a bad student" and after this experience with all of these students together, this proved to me that no matter the inappropriate behaviours of any student, that each of these students have the ability to do just the opposite of what we expect them to base on their individual behaviour plans. I think more times than not, we judge students on their profiles before we get to know them and their experiences. As such as educators we often "label" students incorrectly before getting to know them through rapport and positive relationship building. I have also learned that many of my students have not had positive experiences with the adults in their lives and because of this they do not trust any adult, especially those of us that are in positions of authority. Because of this, is it any wonder that students behave the way they do towards adults? Until trust, rapport, and positive relationships are built with any student, learning of any kind will be moot at best.

This specific time was of importance as all of us teachers in the middle school, including myself, had preconceived notions that by putting all students together, especially those with behaviour issues, would not be successful and not much learning would take place. We thought that *many* of these students would see this as a time out of the regular classroom; a time to not care and to show their inappropriate behaviours to the entire middle school and in front of an audience. However, much to our disbelief, all our preconceived notions did not materialize. Instead, the opposite happened which proves that you can "never judge a book by its cover."

I wanted to share this experience as an educator so that readers and possibly other school educators realise that even the students who show negative behaviours on a regular daily basis in the traditional classroom setting, that these students, when given an opportunity to learn about their culture and Indigenous ways of knowing, and the learning is related to them directly, that any student can learn from an experience such as this one. Further to the Barthes (1975), cited in Kim (2006) states, "Narrative is present in every age, in every place, and in every society, in an almost infinite diversity of forms" (p. 251) such as spoken or written language, fixed or moving images, gestures, fables, history, dramas, stained-glass windows, news items, comics, cinema and more" (p. 180). It is because this story is positive, current, and about Inuit youth, in an Inuit community, where the learning is culturally based, relatable and a fixed image of the preparation of a muskox, that this makes such a positive story to retell.

Experiential Cultural Learning: Out on the Land My Observations as a Participant Observer

———◆━━◆◆◆━━◆———

It was a cold, overcast morning in September 2019. The students from the middle school wing (grades 8 and 9) and all their teachers were about to embark on our Fall, out-on-the-land trip. The school organizes these trips twice in a school year, once in the Fall and once in the Spring. These land trips are part of every student learning from grades 6 to 12 at the school. These experiential learning land trips are essential to learning more about their culture and how to survive out on the land and serve the purpose of keeping their cultural traditions and identity from being forgotten. These land trips allow for all students to take part and assists in their development of working with and through each other as they each have certain tasks/obligations assigned to them that they are responsible for. Students know their responsibilities before they go out on the land. It needs to be noted here that before these land trips can happen there is a lot of time, effort, and extra work involved in organizing such a school event. This is all taken care of with our schools 'Culture Committee.' This committee is formed at the beginning of each school year on a voluntary sign-up basis. Teachers from all grades 6 through 12 signs up and once the number required is reached, that is the team for the year responsible for these activities. Some of the pre-trip preparations include hiring Elders to go out on the land with the students to teach their traditional knowledge and to share their own experience growing up on the land through storytelling. And as Little Bear (2014) explains, "Storytelling is an especially important part of the education process. It is through stories that customs and values are taught and shared" (p. 82). Further, he explains, "All of the knowledge is primarily transmitted from the older to the younger generation through language; consequently, language is of paramount importance" (p. 82).

On this morning we asked that all students who were going (and all of them do take part) to meet in the library for a check-in. This is done to check to see that all students are prepared to go out on the land (having the right clothing for the harsh elements). Once students were checked to see that they had everything required of them, we separated them from those that may need other more suitable clothing for the elements. Once everyone was ready, we assembled on the bus and headed to a place called Blueberry Hill, not far away from the community where the school is located.

Upon arrival at Blueberry Hill, much to my surprise and astonishment, it was as if these students were military trained and in survival mode as they got ready to make their way out on the land. Each student was focussed and disciplined, and they knew what each of their roles were to make their experience positive and meaningful for them. Some students prepared to put together the tent while others began to assemble a fire. The fire has several purposes including a source from which to cook what has been killed on the land, a source of heat to gather around when chilled by the weather; and as a place to gather in a circle to share learnings and to tell stories. I was amazed at just how efficient these students were and diligent in following through on their assigned tasks. What was even more astonishing to me is that even the students who have behaviour issues and often disrupt the learning of others in the classroom, these students were dedicated and completely on task. I asked myself why this was so? The only rational answer I can think of is that because these learning opportunities have cultural relevance, and they activities are related to their identity as Inuit, that this makes the learning relatable and therefore learning takes place effortlessly. I also noticed that when Elders are telling their stories around the fire that all students are actively listening and participating with no behaviour issues at all. When the day was over, we went back to school, unloaded the supplies, and put them away and the students then made their way to the bus for home.

The next day I was even more shocked than the day before when we were out on the land. In the classroom we discussed the experience(s) of all students in class and what they had learned. To my surprise, all students had something to say about their learning from the day and others told me about how much they enjoyed the experience. Many students told me that the Elders are the gatekeepers of their traditional knowledge and that they are proud to be who they are as Inuit. They also told me that more of this type of learning needs to happen within their school and community as it is a 'better way to learn' according to students who took part.

This experience taught me just how much these students value their culture and their identity as Inuit. It is cultural events like these that make the learning experience of each student that much more meaningful. Through firsthand, active participatory, experiential learning, it is students like the Inuit that are more accepting of what it means to learn as its both relatable and fun.

This experience has changed my professional life as I no longer judge students according to ability or their behaviour in school. I think that setting and learning that is culturally relevant to students are two of the biggest factors when it comes to learning for meaning and relevance for students. This event was important for all of us involved as it opened our eyes to the fact that if learning is experiential, meaningful, purposeful, relatable, and fun, then any student can learn and enjoy it at the same time.

I wanted to share this experience as an educator so that other readers, including educators, to set an example that no matter the child, no matter the circumstance of that child, no matter where they come from, none of these things matter when it comes to learning that is meaningful and relevant, especially when it comes to relevancy of their identity as Inuit people. Because this story has been so positive for all involved, therefore it is important to share for all to enjoy and to smile.

These three narrative stories using the genre of autobiography make it even more convincing that narrative is research. And according to Kim (2016), "Narrative is embedded in every aspect of our life" (p. 260). Ochs and Capps (2001), cited in Kim (2016) further argue, "Narrative research should go beyond these central topics and instead explore living narratives as 'a hallmark of the human condition', that is less polished, less coherent, but pervasive in ordinary social encounters" (p. 262). These stories have created within me a more positive outlook of our education system, but more work still needs to be done to make it better. I am deeply honoured to know and learn from the Inuit of Canada.

REFERENCES

Clandinin, D. J. & Connelly, F. M. (1994). Personal experience methods. In N. Denzin & Y. Lincoln (Eds.), *Handbook of qualitative research in the social sciences.* Thousand Oaks, CA. Sage.

Kim, Jeong-Hee. (2016). *Understanding narrative inquiry. The crafting and analysis of stories as research.* Sage.

Little Bear, L. (2014). *Jagged worldviews colliding.* UBC Press.

Wilson, S. (2008). *Research is ceremony: Indigenous research methods.* Fernwood Publishing.

Printed in the United States
by Baker & Taylor Publisher Services